TEGAN AND SARA PRESENT

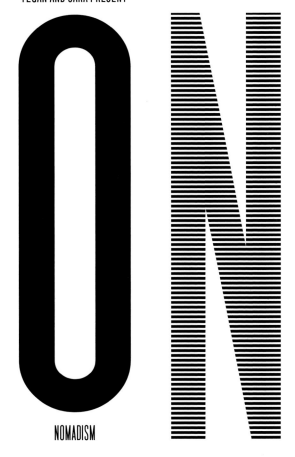

NOMADISM

D1305080

PHOTOS BY LINDSEY BYRNES
ART AND DESIGN BY EE STOREY

PHOTO EDITING LINDSEY BYRNES, EE STOREY

ADDITIONAL LAYOUT BY BRANDON VELESTUK

COPY EDITOR SARAH FOBES

ADDITIONAL COPY EDITING PIERS HENWOOD, KIM PERSLEY

CONTENT MANAGEMENT LINDSEY BYRNES

PUBLISHING COORDINATOR NICK BLASKO

ADDITIONAL PHOTOGRAPHY BY TEGAN QUIN, SARA QUIN, KERRI BORSUK

© *SUPERCLOSE MUSIC, INC.*

ISBN-*978-0-9813192-0-9*

Printed in China

CONTENTS

of ON NOMADISM, A U.S. TOUR with TEGAN AND SARA, OCTOBER 2008

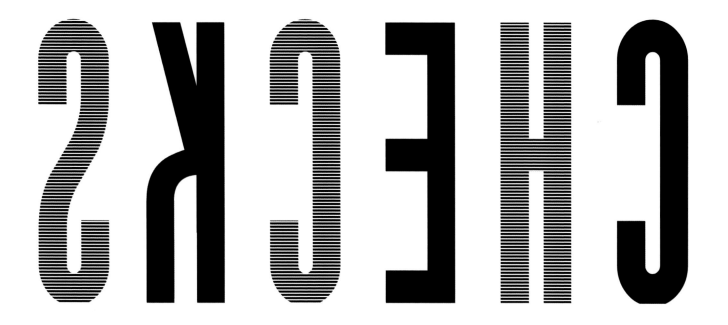

On The Road *by Sonia Clement,* MOM

My father loved to travel. As a child, I spent untold hours in the backseat of our car while he drove endless miles across North America. My mother, his dutiful wife and companion, sat in the passenger seat, assigned with the task of map reading to ensure we reached our planned destinations. Each day, without fail, my dad somehow managed to find the lone farm equipment outpost in each village, town or city that we visited. We would pull into a parking space at these establishments where my mother and I would patiently await his return. Every minute seemed like an eternity, and every time I would plead with him to hurry. These pleas were always met with the assurance of "I'll just be a minute." My mother cleverly utilized this time to do crossword puzzles, and I simply sat and waited, often for much longer than the promised "minute." I remember thinking that I'd never subject my own children to the torture of the tedious and painful experiences misleadingly labeled as "road trips." I didn't know at the time that my formative years would be the preliminary training for what I have since come to know as "going on tour with Tegan and Sara."

As a teenager in the 70's I frequently fantasized about being a rock star. In all of my fantasies, I would imagine myself standing on stage, hearing the adoring screams from my legions of fans. These flights of imagination never included any of the following realities. Traveling from one

venue to the next, waiting for the equipment to be loaded in, the time it takes for the crew to set up the stage, the soundcheck to be called, the set list to be written, the guest list to be finalized, the interviews to be done, the hours spent waiting backstage for the time to pass, the food to be delivered, the venue bathroom that hasn't been cleaned since 1955, and the numerous and mundane tasks that inevitably come with the job as a working musician. That said, the experience of the 90 minutes on stage, the crying and screaming fans, the gracious gifts, and the love? That's powerful stuff, and it really does balance out "the bad."

The first time I traveled with my kids on tour was quite early in their career, and even then the anticipation and excitement was beyond belief. My friends screeched with delight when they heard I was going to go on tour with them. My friends, family and colleagues were captivated by my "what I did on my summer vacation" stories.

The first trip out with my girls brought back the memories of my eight year old self, sitting impatiently in the backseat of my parents' car. I had imagined the trip would be the ideal opportunity for a vacation together, some bonding time with my daughters. I certainly wasn't prepared for them to go into a "road coma" and for me to suffer the same fate. Evidently this was some type of survival technique – something I vaguely recognized but couldn't attach a name to in the moment. Eventually I re-

On The Road *by Sonia Clement,* MOM
CONTINUED

alized that to survive touring you had to become a master of passing time, and as it turned out, that was a skill I had already developed in my childhood from years of traveling with dad.

A decade has passed since the girls started their career and their path has taken many forms, some better than others. A ten passenger van is a significant step up from a minivan with a tent packed in the back. Other improvements include the far less frequent outbursts of "shotgun" and "Sara's touching me!" or "Tegan stole my seat."

I remember the incredible relief I felt when the vans became tour buses, knowing that Tegan and Sara, along with their band and crew, would be safer and far more comfortable on those long road trips. It was with great excitement that I arrived in Phoenix to travel with the girls on their first tour in an actual tour bus. Once again my rock star fantasy was challenged. Who knew such smells could exist? My imaginings had never included tiny stacked bunk beds, or boys and all the smells that come with them. It didn't take long for the girls to incorporate some ground rules in regards to everything, from the handling of smelly socks to a bathroom usage schedule. And in time, life on the bus improved.

There is so much more to say about the life my children lead as musicians, but I will conclude with this thought. In 2004, I accompanied Tegan and Sara to Australia as their "merch girl." I believe we flew 13 times in three weeks. I hated my suitcase, it became unbearably heavy as the days passed. At night, I would contemplate what I could throw away to lighten my load. Over the course of those three weeks, I earned two ear infections, strep throat and a lot of bodily aches and pains. I don't think I have ever been so grateful to go home. Touring is hard work. I think back to that little girl in the back seat of my parents' car and the experiences I had and I realize that all the practice I had daydreaming, disassociating and waiting for my dad could never have truly prepared me for the life of a rock star. I just don't have it in me. I try to visit my kids on tour as often as I can, and when I do go I fly and get my own hotel room. Over the years I have prepared an impressive list of excuses for why I can't go when they ask me to tour with them. Number one on my list? I'm just too old.

After countless years of theory and classical training on the piano, my brain is now too crowded to add guitar theory to the circuitry. I can barely remember the names of the strings, so Ted often has to call out the string and fret when we are working on new stuff. This is my way. I don't re-

member life before Ted and I don't want to think about life after him. That life would consist of me making notes while I write my songs and then trying to remember what the notes meant later on. Yuck.

"Tired of Sex" *by Sara*

In 1996, Weezer released the album *Pinkerton*. I was 16 years old, wearing pants ten times too big and oversized t-shirts plucked straight from my 6'4 stepfather's closet. I had let my hair grow so long that I could have worn it as a winter coat. My favorite moment of every week came on Friday night, when my friends and I, stumbling and crashing into each other, danced and hollered song lyrics into the ceiling above our heads. "Dancing" rarely involved much more than clutching one another's baggy clothing and hopping around aimlessly in pogo fashion, as full albums blared at an outrageous volume. Weezer's "Tired of Sex" was my favorite song that year.

Long after my hair had been mercifully shorn and our career had started its slow build across the border into America, a mutual friend introduced me to Matt Sharp, the bass player from Weezer. Our initial meeting was on-line and he was shy and sweet and I was beyond thrilled to discover that he was aware of our existence.

It's been many years since that first meeting, and we have since toured and performed together countless times. Matt showed us the way when we decided to venture into Moog and keyboard territory on *So Jealous*, and he even picked up the bass again for an appearance on *The Con*. Matt is a dear friend, but I'd never asked him if we could perform my favorite Weezer song on stage together. I would have just been satisfied with a private living room sort of happy accident, after a bottle of wine. But while playing three shows at the Henry Fonda Theater in LA, Matt made my teenage heart leap when he joined us on stage for a cover version of "Tired of Sex." It was thrilling. The word nervous doesn't come close to describing the sensation I felt the first night we attempted to perform the song live. Hands shaking, blood rushing. I imagine myself as that silly teenager, watching from the crowd, and I wish I could go back in time and tell that girl what would eventually happen to her. She would have been psyched.

Small Adventures On Wheels *by Emy*

I started working with Tegan and Sara in the summer of 2003, and from that point forward I've been their art director. I traveled with them selling merchandise through many stages of life and touring, from minivans and tour buses to planes and bicycles. The touring life is punctuated by adventures both distinct and subtle.

I. — MEMORIES OF THE MERCH TABLE

Selling merchandise is a multi-faceted endeavor that I began turning into a circus in 2003. Decorations and lights were the key. For a while, I was customizing old suitcases so that they could be stacked on top of each other, plugged in and lit up to make an telaborate display. Things were so lo-fi and crafty back then! I would hang the t-shirts using wire coat hangers that I'd tape to any surface receptive to adhesive. Eventually we graduated to poles and mounts that I would drape with lights, t-shirts and decorations, and then hoist up to display at a noticeable nine feet. During the *So Jealous* tour we put on fundraisers at the merch table. I bought big swatches of red felt and we cut out thousands of hearts that we sold for a dollar, raising money for charities and community organizations. We had a Lite-Brite, on which Sara would customize a message such as "Hello Pittsburgh" before every show. All these efforts were rewarded because our merchandise enterprise became very successful and at times even out of hand. Sometimes the crowds at the merch table were so big they'd slowly push the tables inward, pinning me up against the wall. The fans were always amazing and interesting. I loved when Tegan and Sara would come out to sign after the show because I'd feel like their bodyguard, which for some reason really excited me. That used to happen a lot back then when crowds were more manageable. Most of the time I ended up being more of a psychological bodyguard. I never had to break any legs.

II. — CAB RIDE IN CHEYENNE

Our hotel in Cheyenne, Wyoming was on the outskirts of the city, so the whole group took a $50 cab ride to the movie theatre across town. I forget what movie we saw, but I do remember the cab ride home. Once the driver found out that he was among musicians, he took it upon himself to share his prose with some fellow artists. The best poem was called "The Crystal Cock." It was about his dick and a crack pipe. This is one of those sacred memories that I wish I could supplement with a slide show.

III. — LUXURIOUS HOTEL IN DETROIT

On show day in Detroit we pulled into the parking lot of a motel where we had reservations. Before we could even step out of the van, a cop car pulled up to us and the cop said, "You're not goin' in there are you? Bad people are in there."

We had to go in because we had eight boxes of merchandise waiting for us in the lobby. The boxes were there, and being used as foot rests by a group of incredibly sketchy, cigar-smoking men. Desperate to shower, we headed upstairs through a crooked hallway with peeling wallpaper and fire-damaged exposed wooden beams. The room itself was straight out of a horror movie. Tegan bolted, but Sara and I tried to make it work. The bathroom was so disgusting that we poured Tide into the tub to clean it, hoping we wouldn't have to touch anything. It was pointless because the tub didn't even drain. We put plastic bags on our feet to walk on the bathroom floor.

IV. — WEST EDMONTON MALL FIASCO

The West Edmonton Mall fiasco is the craziest night I ever worked the merchandise table. West Edmonton Mall is the biggest mall in the world. It has an amusement park, a water park, dolphins, hotels and like 10,000 stores. It's a psychotic retail maze. Before soundcheck, Ted, Sara and I rode the pirate ship ride and Sara almost fell out because she was smaller than the "you must be this size to ride this ride" sign. We were the only ones on it and we screamed and all our change fell from our pockets. That night I sold over 500 t-shirts, got a beer dropped on my head from the balcony above, and chased and caught a kid who tried to steal from me. And then to top it all off, Sara, Craig and I almost got into a fist fight with some manager. This was also the night where Sara traded her shoes for the soon to be legendary red, black and yellow vintage high tops!

V. — BBQ AT MARGO & JOHN'S HOUSE

While on tour, travel days disappear, show days are exciting and packed but blend together, and days off are often the most memorable. In the summer of 2005, we had a day off after a show in Albany, which is close to where I grew up in the small rural town of Kinderhook, NY. So we planned a barbeque at my mom and dad's house. The tour bus and the trailer took up their entire driveway, enthralling the neighbors. Family and friends who made the trip down from Montreal and my amazing 95 year old grandmother attended our backyard party. Sara and I bought a beautiful old bicycle from a trailer park down the street for $40, which we rode around every city we went to from there on until I tried to double her in Nashville, TN and almost got heat stroke.

VI. — ACCIDENTAL CONSUMPTION

As the merch seller I always had to be inside the venue before everyone else. I was also the last one out, since I'd have to pack up, count out, and settle up with the venue. This whole process was very time consuming, so when I wanted to eat I had to do it fast. In accordance with my typical binging tendencies, I had rapidly eaten dinner and was headed off the bus when I spotted a package of delicious looking brownies that a fan had given us at the previous show. I quickly ate two or three before going into the venue. I'd started selling merchandise but was soon on the walkie talkie: "Can somebody bring me a few bottles of water? It's so dry out here!" and "Oh my god the crowd is so weird tonight, everyone is looking at me and no one will talk to me!" and "Seriously I need more water, I think my throat is closing!" and so on and so forth. It wasn't until late that night that Sara simply sniffed the brownies and made the realization that I was completely high. I am so naïve.

VII. — THE L.A. SHOWS, FALL 2008

After being retired from touring for almost two years, I decided that I had to see the last shows of *The Con* tour in L.A. It's weird coming back on the road after you've been away for a while, but walking into the venue it felt like I had never left. I wasn't selling merchandise anymore, that had long been taken over by the fabulous Lindsey Bathke, and yet the feeling of it all flooded back instantly. The four sold-out nights at the Henry Fonda Theatre were incredible. I have seen Tegan and Sara play hundreds of shows yet I could never get tired of watching them perform. I am so proud of them and I love them and everyone who is a part of our organization. To be there with my best friends and all those incredible people, together we keep those wheels turning. It was another adventure among so many memories both small and significant.

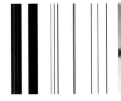

Prop 8 *by Tegan*

When the networks announced Barack Obama had won the presidency, I felt as elated as the rest of the world did. I felt confident that the American people, and more specifically the people of California, would also vote to defeat Prop 8 in one momentous swoop, regardless of all the bright yellow, idiotic "Vote Yes on Prop 8" signs scattered everywhere. While relief rushed over me about the election, initial numbers were showing that Prop 8 was actually going to pass. I was in shock and felt tears welling up in my eyes. Sneaking away to the bathroom, I took a moment to allow a deeply frustrated sadness to come over me. The pinnacle of that sadness came later that night as I lay in bed recognizing that the feeling inside me was shame. Not shame for the people who voted Yes (that would come later) and not shame for people who didn't vote at all (that too would come later), but shame for myself. Shame that I hadn't done more.

It hadn't been enough to talk about it every night on stage to crowds of thousands, or have advocates tabling at the shows. Of course these efforts had an effect, however it was the government that had failed in the first place by putting the question of civil rights to a vote. I thought about a line from a speech by former Canadian Prime Minister Paul Martin, in support of the Civil Marriage Act that legalized gay marriage in Canada: "Our rights must be eternal" he said, "not subject to political whim." I wished I had done more to get this message across.

In the few weeks following the election I managed to refocus the guilt I felt and turn it into pride. Along with tens of thousands of other California residents and visitors, I marched, rallied and blogged in support of the people who had their civil rights taken from them with the passing of Prop 8. I witnessed people from all over the world coming together in support of gay marriage. There is a lot of work to do and a tremendous amount of progress to be made, and I intend to continue to fight to make that change happen.

Tegan And Sara Are Teachers
by Kate from AN HORSE

Last year Sara sent me a picture of herself snowshoeing. She looked brave. In the same email she asked if An Horse would be interested in joining her and her lovely sister Tegan on the road for their "Out of Hibernation" US tour. I said yes, then I rang Damon to tell him. We danced like little girls and began preparations as you would for a school dance. First we talked about our clothes, then we talked about our hair.

So what happens when you go on tour with a band that a) you are a fan of, b) you are friends with, and c) you are approximately the same height as? A whole lot. On the outside you act tough and cool, but on the inside you're scared. Scared of playing to someone else's fans. Scared that those fans will heckle you. Scared that Tegan and/ or Sara will fail to find your antipodean quirks adorable. Scared that they will know when you mess up. Scared that they will think the shirt you wore two nights ago was ugly. Scared that they won't give you back your passports. Ever.

I asked Damon to tell me when he was most scared on tour with Tegan and Sara.

"This one time during the "Out Of Hibernation Tour," I drove our van with Sara sitting in the backseat through a massive snowstorm from Aspen, Colorado to Denver. It was only a few dates into the tour and not long after we'd met. There was a lot of chatter coming from the girls as usual, but I was silent as I struggled to drive through my first ever snowstorm on what for me was the wrong side of the road. All I could think was "You have to get Sara to Denver in one piece or everyone will kill you." It was a nice moment when we all arrived in Denver alive."

It was a very nice moment indeed when we finally arrived. Damon was so busy trying to keep the van on the road that he failed to notice that we'd run out of the anti-freeze that prevents ice from building on your windshield. Trying to see through our windshield was like staring through an ice cube tray. I remember being scared but acting bravely. I think Sara was just as scared but she also acted just as bravely. Her knuckles were white.

Another time I acted bravely on tour was when we played Madison, WI. We arrived in town the night before the show and went out for a civilized dinner. That civilized dinner turned into a civilized game of pool. I lost every game because both Tegan and Sara are vicious pool sharks. After many a game of pool and more than a few drinks, someone thought it might be clever to drink some kind of strong Canadian beer. I remember being brave drinking it.

I remember running down hallways of a hotel. I remember Tegan playing music on her computer. I remember a game of charades. I remember hurting badly the next morning and not being so brave.

We have been lucky enough to play shows with Tegan and Sara in the US, the UK and Australia. I think we know them pretty well. We have learned so much from the girls and their crew. We learned that it's best to have a good two-hour gap between eating dinner and playing and it's best not to order the pulled pork sandwich. We learned to hand over our passports whenever Tegan or Sara asked and that they were not joking about deciding when we can return home. We learned that a hockey bag can fit one person comfortably. We learned a lot about Amish culture. I asked Damon what he had learned from touring with Tegan and Sara.

"For me, they really reinforced that you have to believe in yourself no matter what anyone says about your band, and to always listen to your instincts. Being in a band it's easy to doubt yourself and the music you create, but touring with Tegan and Sara really gave us the confidence to continue. Apart from them being so supportive of An Horse and genuinely believing in us, I absolutely love playing to their audiences. I've toured a lot and supported many other bands yet have never experienced such enthusiastic and supportive fans. The experiences with their fans and the opportunity to see Tegan and Sara play each night was amazing."

I agree with Damon. To completely sum up our tour experiences with Tegan and Sara is hard. They are two of the most generous, fun and supportive people I have ever met. To think that they like our music enough to have invited us on the road several times continues to blow my mind. That they often watch our set with genuine interest is a surreal experience. To know that they really believed in us took some getting used to, but when we saw them in action on tour, and saw the energy that they invest in supporting creativity, it all started to make sense. If everyone in the industry behaved like Tegan and Sara the music world would be a lovely place. And on a side note, we did get our passports back but they know we are willing to surrender them again at any moment.

Johnny

Johnny 5 started playing for Tegan and Sara late in the record cycle for *So Jealous*. He was told we were a subdued, low key band that rarely drank. His first night on the bus we had a raging party that featured a conga line into the bunk area. I'm surprised he stayed. Ted talked him into playing keyboards on a few songs in addition to the drums. Next a keg stand? Unlikely.

Ted

Ted joined the band in early 2004 for the beginning of *So Jealous*. He was supposed to learn two songs from each of our records when he came for try-outs but instead he learned them all. We also liked that he was sporting plaid even though the '90s were way over. Generally he is referred to as MD. "Musical Director." But this does not mean that he makes more money than anyone else in the band.

Shaun

Shaun joined the band for *The Con*. Once he balanced on a yoga ball standing up and juggled for me. Or was that a dream I had? He is the band member who is in the best shape. He also doesn't seem to be too embarrassed or shy to walk around in a bathing suit. Best of all he can play a keyboard bass almost as well as a regular bass, so if we ever outlaw stringed instruments in our band he would not be kicked out. This brings me comfort at night in my bunk.

Chris

Chris Hibbins dresses up to do sound, and we like that. He has also been known to jump off the bus at red lights to get "Scottish Embassy" (McDonalds) for us while we circle the block in anticipation. With us since *If It Was You*, and promising to stay for the long haul, we often refer to Chris as "irreplaceable" behind his back.

Doug

Doug McKendrick sleeps in a top bunk. With all the hours he spends on stage working during the day, you'd think he would demand better real estate. Often after Doug finishes a tour with us he will fly to the furthest place he possibly can to start another job. The reason, among many others, is why we keep having him back.

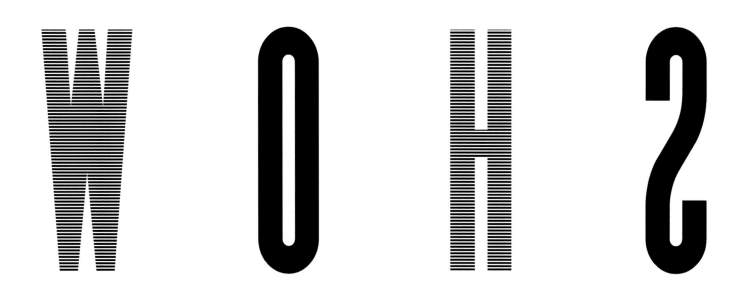

Sometimes I can't believe that these people are really there to see us.

"Teegs" And "Sar"
by Dallas Green of CITY AND COLOUR

Music is everything to me. It helps me breathe. It keeps me awake at night. It can be my best friend and at times, my worst enemy. For the better part of the last decade I have found myself traveling the world solely because I sing and play guitar. To this day, I still find that hard to believe.

One of the best parts about being on tour is that you have the chance to meet people that you most likely would never have come across in normal, everyday life. Sometimes, if the stars align, friendships are born. Fortunately for me, I was lucky enough to meet two of the most amazing girls in the world, who I can now proudly call my friends.

About 10 years ago, I was watching a segment on Much Music called *The New Music*, and these twin sisters from Alberta who had just signed to Neil Young's record label came on. I specifically remember being very envious of the fact that they had signed with Neil Young! They were just two girls who played acoustic guitar and sang, but there seemed to be something more to them than that. Over the years, as I pursued my own career in music, I started to hear more and more about these girls.

In 2004 they released a record called *So Jealous*. After that record, I noticed that a lot of the bands we were touring with were gushing over this group from Canada called Tegan and Sara. Very serious, tattooed metal dudes who listen to metal and dressed and acted like they were in metal bands seemed to love Tegan and Sara. I hadn't yet

fallen in love with them. Not because I wasn't into their music, but because it wasn't my time. But they were always on my mind. Strangely, during one European tour we received several boxes of what was supposed to be our merch but turned out to be mistakenly sent boxes of Tegan and Sara shirts.

Years went by and whether it was hearing that Jack White was a fan or hearing Tegan singing with Against Me!, or just seeing their faces on the covers of magazines I kept hearing about these two girls. I was starting to wonder why we had never met. The Canadian music scene is not a very big one, surely we should have played some sort of festival together by now. I even played a show in Vancouver and heard that Tegan was there, but still, no meeting.

I finally met the magnificent Tegan (or Teegs, which is how I refer to her) in 2008, and within minutes we bonded over a shared experience: we both hate our own songs. A few weeks later I was asked to open for the girls' final tour in support of *The Con*. I was a little nervous about doing it because I had heard rumors that the girls did not get along well with one another, and because Tegan and I had gotten along so well I wondered whether or not Sara would like me. Tegan had also asked me if I would re-work one of their old songs to perform in their encore with them and my first thought was "what if Sara hates it?"

It was in Atlanta, GA where I finally met the wonderful Sara. She was very kind and immediately put me at ease. Since I was traveling with only a merch person, I was essentially on my own. So I just invited myself into the girls' lives and the lives of their amazing band. They

accepted me with open arms and thus began our story. While the opening band was playing, some of the guys from the band noticed the world's largest spider crawling around by their dressing room. I grabbed a cup and cornered it. I trapped it under the cup and wrote a note that read "NEVER TOUCH THIS CUP!" We laughed and I knew we all had the same sense of humor.

Somewhere along the way, I found myself falling in love with Tegan and Sara. We figured out that I was born just ten days after they were, September 29th, 1980. From that point on we decided that I was their long lost brother. This made us triplets. There was something strange about how well we got along and I concluded that we should have already met and been friends a decade earlier and that now we were just making up for lost time. I also started watching them play every night, which was followed by me singing along every night, which was followed by me becoming a super fan.

Everyone, from their crew, to the band members, to the world famous Lindsey and Emy, were absolute pleasures to be around for that month. I experienced some of the most amazing times I have ever had on tour, primarily because of the conversations I would find myself involved in after the shows. Whether it was Sara and I discussing relationship troubles or records that we loved, or the night I told the girls that I would be the surrogate father of their children, every day was amazing and I am so thankful for the opportunity that they gave me. I have been on more tours than I can remember, but I will never forget the time I spent with Tegan and Sara. —Love, Dal

While Tegan and Dallas sing "The First" each night, a song from early in our career, I think of the basement where the words and melody were written. We were 18 years old, just out of high school and paying the rent with minimum wage jobs. Tegan had painted her room purple, and she would play this song in its earliest form early in the morning or well into the night. I remember thinking that it was a song to be proud of. And now, 11 years later, standing side stage, I found a way to like it again.

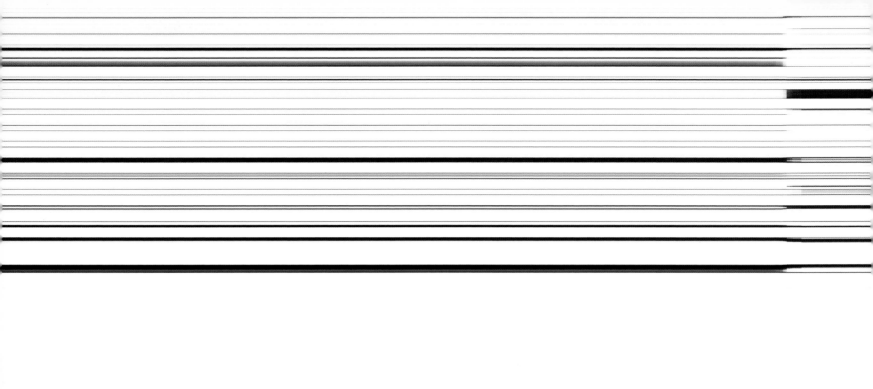

ıch
on
ter

We have officially been a band for over 10 years. This was the first time we had a real light show. This means that people could have been on drugs or wearing 3-D glasses and this would have passed off as a "real" concert with real "lights."

Sometimes in daydreams, but never while on stage, I think about throwing myself into the open flat palms of the audience.

Drummers have the best view. It's too bad we can't afford jumbo screens and full time camera crews. Johnny 5 makes it look easy. And take it from me, it's not easy being a drummer.

What We Learned From Touring With Tegan And Sara *by Spero,* NORTHERN STATE

I. If you thought touring with your two best friends could be a challenge at times, try touring with your twin. Yowza.

II. Canadians are hilarious, and also apologetic. The hallway of the bus was a constant chorus of Canadian voices saying "Surry," "Surry," "No, I'm surry," "No, it is I who is surry." What were they all so "surry" about?

III. Girl musicians have to work hard every day to be respected. We thought maybe it was just us, but as good friends of Tegan and Sara, we watched them struggle at times, in spite of their success, to ensure that their business ideas and creativity are being respected. It ain't always easy, but these girls sure make it look that way.

IV. If you leave the bus bathroom door unlocked while using it, you will get walked in on. No exceptions.

V. Canada is one big-ass country. If you don't believe me, try driving across it. You will be "scanning for moose" for months after, even once you are home in Queens. We were thrilled to be asked by Tegan and Sara to tour Canada with them. It's a land we knew virtually nothing about, despite Canada being our friendly neighbors to the North.

VI. Tegan and Sara were in dire need of nicknames. Enter TT, Sa Sa, Teegs, T-bird, Sa Sa bird, Lil' Sa, Tegano, and so on, and so forth.

VII. Tegan and Sara's fans are the best. Besides Northern State fans, of course. And thankfully, now, some are one and the same.

VIII. Women supporting women is a beautiful thing. We love those crazy hos!![1] When we met Tegan and Sara, neither they, nor we, had ever done any substantial touring with another female band. Tegan and I talked about this the first time we met, and knew it had to be corrected immediately. Fast forward several years, and we are so grateful for the support they have shown to our band, and for their rock-solid friendship.[2] If Tegan and Sara quit music tomorrow and decided to open a bakery, we'd be the first ones in line.

---

[1] *Tegan and Sara are not, and have never been, hos.*

[2] *I am getting so emotional typing this, I'm going to "phone" Tegano right now!* [3]

[3] *Canadians say "phone," not "call."*

Al

Al is the guitar tech. This means he comes on stage and hands us guitars that he has tuned between songs. His job puts him in high stress situations almost constantly. In addition to tuning guitars, loading and unloading the trailer, setting up the stage and tearing down the stage and tuning both Sara's and my guitars, and doing maintenance and string changes on them, he is also responsible for clearing the stage of bras, fan letters and teddy bears. People ask Al to give them our guitars sometimes after we finish the show when he is working on stage, and he tells us all about it later after he loads out and we are on the bus. Al used to work at a hotel and sometimes I get scared he'll go back to his old job there. When I tell him this he laughs.

These people are easier to face than the smallest gathering or a house party. We're a team. I've never performed under the influence of drugs or alcohol. What would be lost if this picture were out of focus?

W

T

F

Sara and I don't touch often. We have many theories for this. Once someone smart theorized that perhaps we were too biologically similar to come that close without becoming one. That's some sci-fi shit! I'm not sure if I believe it but I adhere to it just in case.

There is relief at the end of a show, but there is also a
desire to stand and wave until every last person is gone.

Sometimes at night after our set, Tegan and I go back to the "day room" and dig through the pile of wet used towels and order cake from room service.

This is the one and only time I can remember us ever doing this. It was a tiny hotel room, after midnight and I have just hogged down pizza and ice cream. I was desperate to lay down. On any other occasion I would have stood rather than been caught on film on a bed with Sara.

Seriously. Room service.

Hotels: *Lindsey Bathke's Rules For Entry*
PART I

Upon entry, I place my key near the door as to not forget it when heading out. If it is a grand deluxe room, like in Australia, I place my bags at the door, allowing me to further explore the place at ease. I then choose which room I will take, trying to let Chris have the bigger room, due to seniority. If it is a smaller room, like in America, I usually choose the bed furthest from the door, because I don't want to be the first one killed if someone enters.

After choosing a room or a bed, I bring my suitcase to the end of the bed or put it up against a wall. I try not to get too close to the bed because I think bed bugs will know and awaken from their slumber to explore what new items I have brought into the room. My suitcase folds in half, so I always fully unzip it, making sure both sections are flat on the floor. I always place my backpack away from the bed, usually with the pockets facing the wall, so that its contents do not spill out when I keep it open.

I love inspecting the free toiletries you get in hotel bathrooms, and I generally feel disappointment if there is no lotion provided. I have a thing about miniature versions of products. I love them. I usually bring my two toiletry bags into the bathroom. I have one for shower items and one for out-of-shower items. I like to leave them in the bathroom because it feels more like home. Neither toiletry bag is placed anywhere near the toilet! I had a friend in college who would not bring her toothbrush near the toilet because she thought when she flushed, all the germs would spray from the toilet and grab onto your toothbrush.

Hotels: *Lindsey Bathke's Rules For Entry*
PART II

Before I sit on the bed, I pull the blanket back. Often, what you can see on the underneath blanket is worse than what you can't see on the top one. I never place any clothes on the bed, unless I have the sheet exposed. I do not want bed bugs to travel with me. I sometimes pull up one of the corners of the mattress to check for bugs, but it's a yucky thing to do, cause what if you find them... moving rooms it is! It should be a general rule not to put any clothes or bags close to the bed.

Sometimes I consider taking a bath in the hotel room once I arrive, in order to help relax. Then I think about all the other bums that sat in that same tub, so I usually opt for a shower instead.

While sleeping, I never let the outer blanket touch my arms or any exposed skin, if I have chosen to keep that outer blanket on the bed. I try not to think about how filthy the carpet might be because I like to take off my shoes. I like to wipe off the remote control before use, or I feel like my fingers are coated with grime. Germs and bacteria love remote controls. Germs also love drinking glasses because maids barely wash the glasses other than giving them a meaningless rinse in the sink. For that reason, I love the disposable plastic cups wrapped in plastic, as seen at the Holiday Inn. If it is glass, I will try to clean the edges of the glass with my fingers and some water, just to fool my mind.

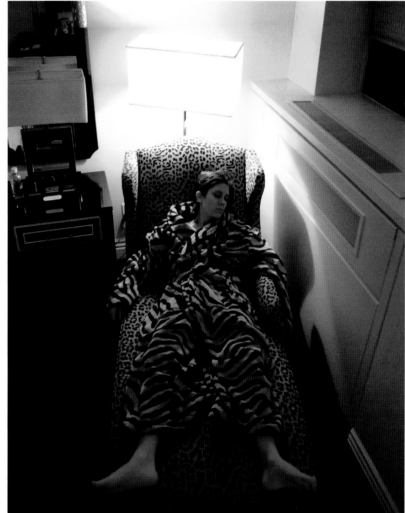

I don't know what I was reading here but chances are it was
fiction and involved themes including but not limited to:
death, love, ballet, and the facts of life.

Tegan wants to get gay married again and again and again.

It felt like a lucky break to be touring the month leading up to the US Presidential Election in November 2008. The only downside to this is that most of the debates were scheduled right when we were going on stage. Damn us for playing so early. We're such sissies. This particular photo we are watching the only Vice Presidential debate and my cousin Chelsea, who lives in Washington, watched it with us. I had moments where I felt a little guilty for caring so much about the US election when we ourselves had an election only a few weeks earlier in Canada, but I knew that Tim Horton would win so I didn't feel as compelled to watch.

I can do amazing things to kill time. And I wonder why my eyes droop. This should be an advertisement for ptosis. Do this and lose your ability to hold your eyelids up! Don't be like me.

This pizza came from a movie theater. This is not where you should get pizza. You get popcorn at a movie theater. It was cold and only partially cooked but I ate it anyway, because the person who had cooked it was watching us. I need to get a backbone.

Nighttime eating on the road has the potential to be incredibly disgusting. In one's youth, it is relatively consequence free to eat carcinogenic, chemical-filled packaged food in massive quantities. As the body ages, it begins to reject this kind of nourishment. While on the road we are given restaurant menus before soundcheck. We make a chart with our selections. There is a sense of anticipation that the food may actually be good, and of course, the expectation that it will be mediocre. Berries and other explicitly healthy foods are delivered to our dressing room in a separate order from our dinners. By the end of the night everyone chugs red bulls and eats chips.

My house never looks like this. If my coffee table were covered with this much food, I would twitch until every tiny crumb was removed with a cleaning product.

The first time we did TV in America was *The Late Show with David Letterman*. This was back in 2001. I wore an extremely tight Tim Hortons t-shirt which I immediately regretted. This time I wore my "sad suit" and favorite shirt at the moment and felt I looked quite cute and was totally happy with the performance. Being on a show so familiar and popular makes you feel like reality and fantasy are crashing into each other. No matter how much or how little make up they put on us I still feel like we look like we're not actually there, but in fact dropped in later in post production or something like that.

My parents each have an extensive library of photo albums documenting every year of our lives. Every bad hair cut, every horrible outfit, every awkward stage and every ridiculous birthday party has been captured on film. Bruce, our Stepdad, painstakingly ordered the photos in the albums according to the negative. As musicians we have to get our photos taken all the time. We are well prepared for this from all that childhood training.

Tour Bus Etiquette *by Tegan*

The tour bus, even in theory, always scared me. Even though I truly hated sitting in the back of a van for six years, I still had a hard time envisioning life on a tour bus. Our first tour bus was experienced in Europe in 2003 and it was a double decker. We were sharing with fellow Canadian band Hot Hot Heat. They had been on the bus for a few weeks and so they had already picked bunks and "expanded" when we arrived. I will never forget packing for that tour and the anxiety that came with trying to figure out what to bring on the tour bus. How would packing for a tour bus in Europe be different than preparing luggage for a 15-passenger van in America?

Would the band we were sharing with like us? Would we get along? Would my girlfriend break up with me because she was uncomfortable with me sharing a bus with 12 men/boys for three weeks? Would I be able to sleep at all? Would we die in a fiery crash somewhere in Germany? How would my mom recover?

The first and most significant image I have of the bus was when we first laid eyes on it. Hot Hot Heat's tour manager was standing outside the bus door without any shoes on, drinking coffee from a camping mug. This bothered me tremendously. The whole thing just didn't seem clean. Even from outside. Hot Hot Heat were very nice and hospitable and I don't remember having any major issues with them beyond the way they hung their show clothes upstairs after they played. The clothes were extremely sweaty and laundry facilities were hard to come by and so they smelled very bad from what I remember.

Towards the end of the tour I was in my bunk with my girlfriend trying to fall asleep when Paul, the drummer, came in after the show and changed clothes right in front of my curtain. Both my girlfriend and I were terrified because we were pretty sure he didn't know we were there, and our deep concern was that he might accidentally move our curtain, thereby accidentally exposing his genitalia to us. This would have made it the second time I'd seen him in this compromising position. On night one on the bus I bumped into him coming up from the bathroom as he was coming down. He was wearing leopard print underwear that I'm pretty sure was of the thong variety.

Touring in North America years later with our own band is a totally different experience. Everyone is expected to wear pajamas or put on clothes to go to the bathroom if they sleep partially undressed. No wandering around in underwear or unnecessary groin scratching is allowed. Ever.

The toilet seat is to be put down and it is preferred

that you pee sitting down regardless of what you have between your legs.

Even a small child is capable of closing the bunk doors that separate the sleeping area from the living area without waking up everyone on the bus. We try to encourage everyone to apply a little bit of effort and consideration when opening and closing bunk doors.

Lastly, there are no hanging, sweaty clothes allowed anywhere. Our bus smells as good as can be expected while living with 12 people in such a tiny space.

Who Cares?

I like to talk

about myself

BlaBlaBla

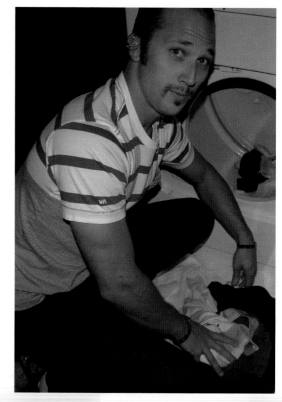

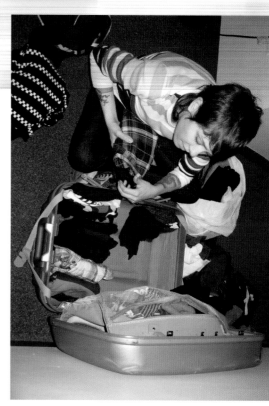

I don't fall asleep until my bag's contents are folded perfectly and color coded. There is a whole system to packing. Rolling of clothes, each tiny package in identical shapes. Every item is partially visible so that a complete inventory can be taken with a simple glance.

To Live Out Of A Bag *by Sara*

I am extremely picky about my belongings and my space. I like everything to be color-coded and stacked in even piles. Compartments, zippers, contained, controlled. This is how we live. No matter how organized I feel, I rarely experience true, organized calm. I stack and refold. I buy new suitcases that seem more efficient. I consider garment bags and coat hangers. I consider one piece jumpsuits or a tour where I only wear one uniform from start to finish. I consider throwing away anything I haven't worn to save space for books and shoe boxes. Sometimes I use my suitcase for sitting on, in airports or hotel lobbies. Occasionally I hate my suitcase. I stare at it in the corner of my hotel room and loathe it, as though its mere existence is just more blinding proof that I live like a strange nomad.

I roll my clothes into tight little packages, leaving no mystery as to the contents stuffed below the top layers of a traditionally packed suitcase. I think about the suitcase's insides, intestinal material that smells like bounce dryer sheets and gas fumes, bouncing from bus to hotel, up stairs and across stages, into the guts of airplanes and into the arms of my tour manager. It's the most vulnerable part of my external body. What would I do if it was lost? I am currently not living out of a suitcase yet I still wander into luggage stores to have a look at the newest contraptions that may soon enough be home to my priceless belongings.

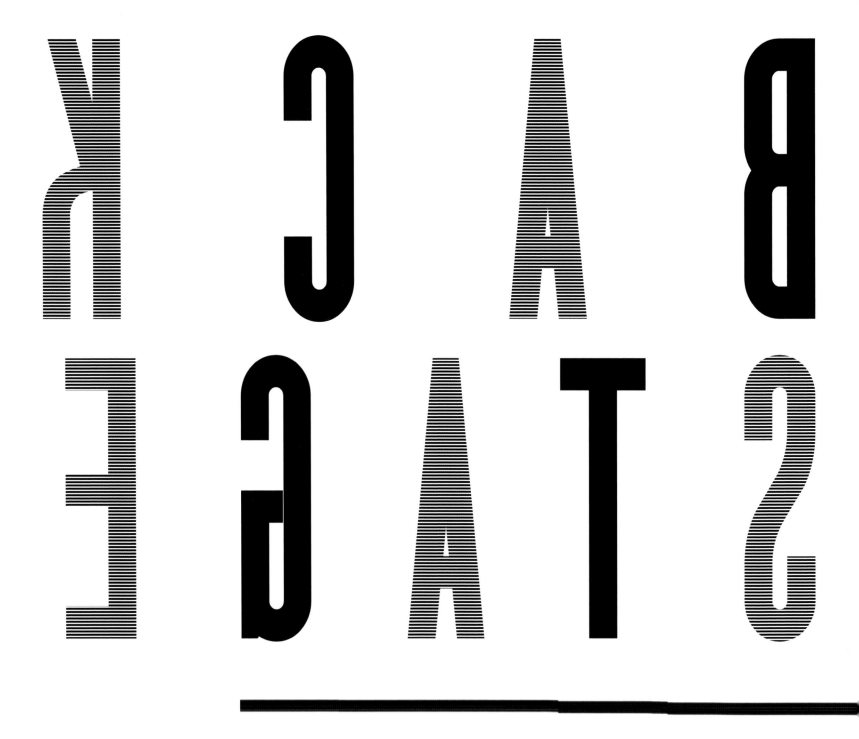

Backstage areas are like hotel suites that are occupied exclusively by musicians and subsequently never get maid service. They are dark and most often grimy. There is traditionally a lot of phallic graffiti. We eat there. We do press there. We wait there. Sometimes we even have to shower there, God help us. We are picky and clean. I think that as the number of women in bands grows there will be a shift in the state of many backstage areas, away from the conventional male filth hole aesthetic.

These photos were taken backstage at the Riviera in Chicago. Here we are discussing doing our new record with Chris Walla.

Tegan And Sara's *Rules Of The Road*

I. Respect the daily schedule at all times (load-in, soundcheck, quiet time, band time, show time, load-out, curfew and bus call).

II. 15 minutes of quiet band time pre-show (The five band members ONLY).

III. 5 minutes of quiet time post show (same as above).

IV. No drinking for band or crew before or during the show.

V. No drugs ever please. No exceptions.

VI. Break down gear and help load out before you leave or start drinking.

VII. Load in and out is for everyone.
Someone will let you know in cases where you are not needed.

VIII. If you are leaving the club or bus please let someone know.

IX. No shoes on in the bus.

X. Keep personal items in your bunk, a junk bunk, a drawer or a closet.

XI. Bus curfew unless otherwise noted is 2am.

XII. Please do not bring guests on the bus after curfew.

XIII. If you bring guests on the bus for a visit, remind them to take their shoes off and to be aware that others may be sleeping depending on the time.

XIV. Try to clean up after yourself when you leave the hotel, bus, van or backstage area.

Over the past 10 years we have gotten some very intense and very awesome stuff from fans. For example: Made-to-scale duct tape replicas of our foot wear. Cakes, cookies and homemade treats, sometimes right out of the oven. Homemade t-shirts, sweaters, hoodies, scarves, hats, pillows and bras with photos of us on them. One of the most amazing gifts was a board game relating to our career with the five band members as playing pieces. We ran wild with that shit.

Once Sara and I were crossing Canada in the freezing winter and we both had colds and we slept in the bus station. At one point I looked over at Sara and she was sleeping sitting up, with her face pushed into her bag which was on her lap. I felt alone and cold. Things have changed so much since then. Now we sleep in little bunks and we wait with the whole band rather than just with each other.

Flagstaff, AZ. Day off. Cold but clear. I am very happy and about to say so as this photo is being taken with the Voigtlander.

Dallas Green is our third part. Put a beard on me and tell
me we don't look related?

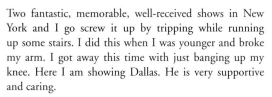

Two fantastic, memorable, well-received shows in New York and I go screw it up by tripping while running up some stairs. I did this when I was younger and broke my arm. I got away this time with just banging up my knee. Here I am showing Dallas. He is very supportive and caring.

Life After Being On The Road
by Tegan

Life at home is very similar to life on the road. The main difference being that at home I don't have a grown man posting a list telling me what needs to get done each day. I am a grown woman who is more than capable of taking care of her own basic needs, but after living as a group for so long there is no "I" left in me.

When I'm home I do my best to stay motivated. I go for walks and read and follow a firm bedtime and wake-up time schedule. I do this so as not to become too lethargic or hermit-like, as these bad habits only make living as a group more difficult when I am back on tour after months of being home.

On the road you have the rest of the group to compare yourself to. For example, has Ted been on his computer as long as I have? If so, I don't feel bad about being on my computer for so long. Has Shaun eaten pizza two days in a row? Me too, so I'm in good company. Is Johnny watching a third episode of *Sopranos* right now? I guess I can too. At home, with no one to compare myself to, I am left in a state of uncertainty when it comes to the simplest things. Is 2pm too late to get up? I find myself wondering at what time the other band members got up? You see what I mean.

So, besides having no set list of things to do, and no one to compare myself to, it's all the same. Late bed time. Late start time in the morning. Music in the middle of the day and again at night. A lot of snacking and grazing out of the fridge. No shoes in the house unless no one is watching. Sheets washed once a week. Same outfit pretty much every day.

The Photos You See Here *by Lindsey Byrnes*

I was in 4th grade when I belonged to my first and last Girl Scout troop. My step-mom, Carol, has always believed in me and when it was time for me to get ready for my first and only Girl Scout camping trip, her trust in me did not falter. My very serious, very scary troop leader was sent over the edge by Carol's confidence in my nine year-old packing abilities and my subsequent failure to pack all of the necessary items, in particular a flashlight and bug spray. I'm sure that despite my memory loss, that experience is to blame for my Over Packing Disorder (O.P.D.)

Whether I am going somewhere for five days or a month, the packing process for me begins about a week before actual time of departure and can be easily divided into two parts. The first is mental preparation and the second is the actual act of packing, which can span over several days. During the whole process I go through various stages of anxiety until the very last minute at which point my anxiety turns into panic. Going on the road as the tour photographer with Tegan and Sara was no exception. I was a mess before I left, but once I arrived in Baltimore and joined the tour I was relieved to garner not even one strange look or comment regarding the amount of bags I had in tow; those wouldn't come until later.

My mission was clear and the goal was to shoot from Tegan and Sara's perspective, focusing on the moments that their audience doesn't see, including the audience themselves.

What we have here is a stripped-down, real account of life on the road. The long drives, the hours between breakfast, lunch and dinner, the soundchecks and the actual performances, as well as the day-to-day living; waiting, reading, packing, unpacking, sleeping, eating and the fun that happens just about everywhere.

This was one of the best experiences of my life. Not just because of the amazing people I was with or the fun I had, but because I think the journey may have cured my O.P.D. In New York City I left a bag in the back of a van cab. Thanks to Tegan's impressive athleticism, and New York's intensely backed up traffic, the bag was recovered. I proved myself to be a much more conservative packer on future tours, but that's another book.

I'm not sure how I feel about this photo. I also have no idea where it was taken. I know it was in America. I look like someone who has a brown belt in karate. It just so happens that I have a brown belt in karate.

Not only do photographers love taking photos, they secretly LOVE having their photo taken. Seconds before I took this photo Lindsey picked up a praying mantis and carried it around to show us. She is a freak when it comes to bugs. No fear. Like those t-shirts in the '90s.

How Touring With Tegan And Sara Is (And Is Not)
Like Summer Camp *by Sprout from* NORTHERN STATE

IS

BUNKBEDS

At summer camp I always preferred the top bunk. I always thought it was because of the view and that it was more exciting to climb into a bed. Top bunk also lacked the claustrophobia of bottom bunk. What I learned on the tour bus was that all of the bunks are claustrophobic and that it's not that exciting (or easy) to climb into your bunk whether it's on top or on the bottom. That said, I still prefer the top bunk. Perhaps it's still because of the view. At summer camp all campers are segregated by gender. Girls bunks. Boys bunks. This was also how we were organized on the tour bus. All of the male crew and band members of Tegan and Sara were up towards the front of the bus and the females were in the back. This made for less awkward accidental moments of seeing people getting in and out of bunks in their skivvies.

RULES

At summer camp there were a lot of rules and we spent our time figuring out which ones were made to be broken; like sneaking out of our cabins and going on raids in the middle of the night. On the Tegan and Sara tour bus there are also a lot of rules, and none of these are meant to be broken. Most of the rules worked well and appealed to my inner neat freak, rules like not being allowed to leave your crap laying around in the common areas of the bus, and not being allowed to wear outdoor shoes inside the bus, and keeping your own items inside of your own bunk with the curtains closed for a tidier look. There were other rules that I wasn't a huge fan of at the time but frankly there were just so many rules it's hard to remember what they all were. Tegan and Sara run a pretty tight ship.

EVENING ACTIVITY

At summer camp there was some kind of organized evening activity that involved large groups of campers. Sometimes there was even a performance in the amphitheater with music and dancing and/or drama. Pretty much exactly the same routine as being on tour. It was always amazing to look out onto the side of the stage and see Tegan and/or Sara watching our set throughout the tour. They are fans of our music, and our message. Over the years of touring together and getting to know each other better, we have become friends and it's been amazing to have the support and friendship of such inspiring and talented musicians. We are huge fans of their music and also of them as people. I loved watching parts of their show every night and I never got sick of the songs or seeing them both up on stage. It was all very magical. Just like summer camp.

IS NOT

ORGANIZED SPORTING ACTIVITIES

There were no organized sporting activities on tour with Tegan and Sara. The closest we ever came to that was Spero and I doing our 'slim in 6' DVDs on our laptops. I heard a rumor that on their next tour, Tegan and Sara purchased street hockey equipment and kept it on the bus and whenever possible would organize a game of street hockey outside the venue before the show. While I cannot confirm or deny this rumor, it does seem quite Canadian and possible, although I cannot really picture Tegan or Sara playing street hockey. I can, however, picture them in bathing suits at the water park in the West Edmonton Mall where they forced us to go on terrifying water slides in our bikinis.

REVEILLE / LINE-UP

At camp we were awoken each morning at 7:30am to the sound of music and asked to line up to raise the flag and hear the announcements for the day. On tour with Tegan and Sara I never really knew what time to wake up – or when we would be arriving at our next city – so I often spent my mornings looking out the window of my top bunk. Sometimes Tegan and Sara were woken up early and whisked away to a hotel to shower and get ready for a full day of press before soundcheck. Other days Tegan and Sara would roll into the venue in their pajamas with their hair all crazy. Northern State pretty much rolled that way all the time.

GHOST STORIES

We did not tell ghost stories on tour with Tegan and Sara. We also did not freeze anyone's bra who fell asleep first, or put warm water on anyone's hand to see if they would pee in their pants, or put shaving cream on anyone's nose to see if they would rub it all over their face.

Sara has recently started walking out on stage at the beginning of the show with her guitar. I am not sure I think this is cool. I can't recall if it is "on" when she walks out or just in her hands. I think "off" is less cool but probably safer if she stumbles in the dark.

"It Could Happen To You" *a MAD LIB by Hesta Prynn*, PH.D.

It is 4AM somewhere in the _____ (LOCATION) countryside. A tour bus speeds over the hills when suddenly and unexpectedly a loud crash is felt, jostling the members

of _____ (CANADIAN TWINS) and _____ (NYC HIP HOP TRIO) awake from their dreams. "Holy _____!!" (EXPLETIVE) says _____ (MEMBER OF TRIO). "What the _____ (EXPLETIVE) was

that?!?" _____ (YOUNGER TWIN), having been launched out of her bunk and into the aisle, notices a _____ (COLOR) bruise developing on her _____ (BODY PART) and goes downstairs

to find out wtf is going on. At this point everyone starts to _____ (VERB) _____ (ADVERB) when _____ (TOUR MANAGER) informs them that their _____ driver has

fallen _____ (NOUN) at the _____ (ADJECTIVE)! "Oooooh _____!!!!" (GENDER) _____ (MEMBER OF TRIO) exclaims while allowing herself to do some _____ (ADJECTIVE)

eating and drinking of a Diet _____ (POPULAR SOFT DRINK) though she had sworn off it on Christmas due to it being made of _____ (TOXIN). Meanwhile, _____ (ELDER TWIN)

is wasting no _____ (NOUN) and has started to dial _____ (MANAGER) on her cell _____ (NOUN). Suddenly and without provocation all _____ (PLURAL NOUN) come to rest on the members

of _____ (TRIO). "Seems like _____ (ADJECTIVE) have brought their _____ (ADJECTIVE) driving _____ (ANOTHER WORD FOR KARMA) to _____ (CONTINENT) with them!" _____ (TWIN) de-

clares. This causes _____ (MEMBER OF TRIO) to become immediately _____ (EMOTION). "Look, anyone can get in ____accidents while touring _____ (WEIRD COUNTRY TO THE NORTH OF THE US). It was a _____ (EXPLETIVE) (#)

_____ (SEVERE WEATHER CONDITION THAT MIGHT CAUSE NYC HIP HOP TRIO TO GET IN 3 CAR ACCIDENTS, WHAT?) for _____ (WESTERN DIETY)'s sake!" "Don't look at me!" _____ (DIFFERENT MEMBER OF TRIO) says.

I don't even know how to _____ (VERB)!" "At least we're all safe." _____ (T+S GUITAR PLAYER) points out. "Yeah, if that _____ (THING THEY PUT ON SIDE OF ROAD SO YOU DON'T DRIVE OFF OF A CLIFF) hadn't been there we all

might have _____." (PAST TENSE VERB) _____ (T+S DRUMMER) adds. "Then we never would be able to tell everyone how much fun we had on this _____" (NOUN) _____ (QUIN TWIN) realizes. "And we

never would have become best _____!!" (PLURAL NOUN) everyone says in unison. Everyone begins to _____ (VERB) and _____ (VERB), grateful for their friendship and their

new lease on _____ (NOUN) when suddenly _____ (T+S BASS PLAYER) and _____ (T+S MERCH GAL) appear on the stairs. "What happened?" they ask. Turns out they had _____ (VERB) ed

through the whole thing!

Our pre-show circle is unlike any one you may have seen on television or in *Truth or Dare*. We have a staring contest and then recite lines from *Arrested Development* or *The Office* the entire time. Basically our band is like a bunch of really rad 16 year olds hanging out unchaperoned.

I think we all "get" each other. Musically and otherwise. Look at our coordination as a band. We could have easily been on *The Breakfast Club* or *Degrassi*.

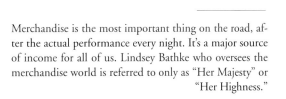

Merchandise is the most important thing on the road, after the actual performance every night. It's a major source of income for all of us. Lindsey Bathke who oversees the merchandise world is referred to only as "Her Majesty" or "Her Highness."

Tips For Australians Touring In America
by Damon from AN HORSE

I. Talk slowly and speak clearly. Sometimes I have to say my name with a slight American accent to avoid being called 'Diamond.'

II. Don't drive tired. One night in Phoenix I was driving home from a show at three in the morning on the wrong side of the road. On another night Kate drove tired through some mountains in Northern California and nearly drove off the side.

III. Always use GPS and always give it a girl's name. Never talk badly to the GPS, as she will turn on you. She holds all the power. Once in Cincinnati I was alone with 'Lily' and I was a little unkind to her. She responded by taking me the wrong way down a one-way street.

IV. Always visit In-n-Out Burger when in California, Nevada or Arizona.
Never use a rest stop that has "Clean this filth hole up" scrawled on the door.
Find an alternative. If this means your pants, so be it.

V. Never let a tour manager or bandmate pressure you into taking any medicine before a 14 hour drive that may deem necessary more of the aforementioned bathroom rest stops.
Do not listen to their health horror stories. Tour managers and bandmates are not qualified health experts.

VI. American toilets flush violently. Secure valuables and make sure you are holding something that is firmly fastened to the floor before flushing.

VII. People will ask you if you knew Steve Irwin, the Crocodile Hunter.
Always answer yes. This should put an end to the conversation.

Matt Sharp is a guru of sorts, from his aesthetic choices (frames) to the core of our tunes (songs).

People imagine the world backstage to be full of a lot of exciting people and things. At least the crazies that break backstage seem to think this as they look highly amped up when they get backstage and then totally disappointed instantly to find us only taking photos of ourselves or trolling the internet for interesting celebrity news before we play. Here is an example of us keeping ourselves entertained backstage....we are talking to each other and taking photos while we do that.

The line up. Sometimes you are there before the sun comes up. We used to be just like you. Tegan and I slept on the pavement out front of Marlborough Mall in 1996 to secure tickets to see the Smashing Pumpkins. Our mother kept a careful watch from the sanctuary of our 1989 Aerostar minivan. It's a jungle out there.

SARA'S QUESTIONS FOR
PROSPECTIVE EMPLOYEES

I. What is your preferred sleeping attire?

II. Do you play organized sports?

III. If you were alone in your house and you were going to dance around or sing passionately in front of your stereo, what album would you put on?

IV. How tall are you?

V. Have you ever been in a fight?

VI. Do you have a gun?

VII. Do you like British TV?

VIII. Do you have a drinking problem?

IX. Are you comfortable taking direction from women? (my Mom and Aunt Julie occasionally like to do a "feelings check" with our tour managers when one of us gets whooping cough that turns into pneumonia)

X. If everyone is grumpy and slow moving and upset, what do you do to make it better?

XI. If we get bad sexist homophobic press and start crying, what do you do?

XII. Do you talk a lot or are you a quiet sniper type? Do you only wear black cut off shorts, accessorized with a carabiner full of keys?

TEGAN'S QUESTIONS
FOR PROSPECTIVE EMPLOYEES

I. Are you a morning person?

II. How tall are you?

III. Do you have sisters?

IV. What's your Mom's middle name?

V. Longest relationship?

VI. Dog or cat owner?

VII. If I asked you to get me a sandwich would you throw it at the back of my head upon your return?

VIII. If I asked you to carry my bag for me up three flights of stairs would you later kick the bag down the stairs in plain view of our merchandise person?

IX. Let's say I owed you a dollar but I chose to "get you back" in smiles instead. How much leeway would you give me on that?

X. Let's say you're checking us in for an international flight and two fire exit seats become available. There are 10 of us flying...who would you give those two seats to?

Lindsey captures the complete experience of Sara's bag packing. Shaun and Chris look on. Everyone is amazed and entertained. It's the little things backstage that keep us sane and happy.

There have been times over the years when I would have described my choice to make music and subsequently tour as just that, a choice. Other times it's more like a compulsion, an itch in need of a scratch. When I'm home I'm antsy to get back on the road. When I'm on the road after a few weeks I'm homesick and dying to get home. Sometimes I describe what we do and why we do it to people and it sounds like I'm describing an addiction. How else do we justify leaving our homes, our friends, our families and our partners, for months at a time year after year? Is it the fans? The money? The fame? The power? The attention? The lists and the organization required each day? The sameness of every day? The ever-changing scenery? The travel? The excitement? The solitude of it all? What is it? My answer is that it's all of those things.

It's every single thing you could imagine that would make it worth it, and then a million more things that you would just have to experience to understand. Growing up we moved all the time. There were so many terrible things that came with moving. The most obvious being changing schools and friends. But there were so many things to look forward to as well. A new room to decorate and organize. A new neighborhood to explore. Touring is sort of like that for me. For every reason not to do it, there are a hundred more why it ends up being worth it. It's hard and it's dirty and often times doesn't pay as well as it seems it should. But every night when I crawl into my little bunk on the bus along with eleven of my closest friends and family, I remember why I do this. It's fun. And that makes it all worth it.